ISRAEL AND THE PALESTINIANS

PAIDEIA
PRESS

ISRAEL AND THE PALESTINIANS

WILLEM J. OUWENEEL

Translated and edited by
Nelson D. Kloosterman

www.paideiapress.ca

Israel and the Palestinians, by Willem J. Ouweneel
Translated and edited by Nelson D. Kloosterman

A publication of Paideia Press (3248 Twenty First St., Jordan Station, Ontario, Canada L0R 1S0).

© 2023 by Paideia Press. All rights reserved.

Scripture quotations are from the ESV® Bible (The Holy Bible, English Standard Version®), © 2001 by Crossway, a publishing ministry of Good News Publishers. Used by permission. All rights reserved. The ESV text may not be quoted in any publication made available to the public by a Creative Commons license. The ESV may not be translated in whole or in part into any other language.

All rights reserved. Except for brief quotations in critical publications or reviews, no part of this book may be reproduced in any manner without prior written permission from Paideia Press at the address above.

Cover Art and Book Design by Steven R. Martins

ISBN 978-0-88815-345-6

Printed in the United States of America

Table of Contents

Foreword | 7
Thesis 1 | 9
Thesis 2 | 13
Thesis 3 | 17
Thesis 4 | 21
Thesis 5 | 23
Thesis 6 | 27
Thesis 7 | 29
Thesis 8 | 31
Thesis 9 | 35
Thesis 10 | 39
Thesis 11 | 41
Thesis 12 | 45
Thesis 13 | 49
Thesis 14 | 53
Thesis 15 | 57
Thesis 16 | 59
Thesis 17 | 63
Thesis 18 | 65
Thesis 19 | 67
Thesis 20 | 69
Afterword | 73

FOREWORD

THE DISCUSSION about the Palestinian-Israeli conflict has reignited everywhere due to the war in Israel and Gaza that broke out on October 7, 2023. On one side, in our country, "progressive" parliamentarians advocate for the impoverished Palestinians, and "modern" theologians protest with a manifesto what they see as objectionable Israeli policies. On the other side, many Christians emphasize the biblical "land promise" for the people of Israel and stand up for the right of the state of Israel to defend itself. Still others are perplexed by the extraordinary complexity of the issue.

The current debate is a good opportunity to try to clarify the relationships between Jews and Arabs based on twenty theses.

We extend our thanks to the website cvandaag.nl, where a large portion of these theses was previously published (though without the explanations provided below). I'm happy to recommend this Christian website for news and discussions about Israel and the Israeli-Palestinian conflict.

I also thank Dr. Perry Pierik of Aspekt Publishing, who proposed that I compile the previously published theses into a small booklet.

Dr. Willem J. Ouweneel
(retired professor of systematic theology)
Loerik (near Houten, Netherlands)
November 4, 2023 (exactly four weeks after the start of the war between Israel and Hamas)

THESIS 1

The word "Palestinian" means a resident of Palestine, regardless of his/her origin. Up until the 1950s, the Jewish residents of Palestine were also called "Palestinians." Conversely, the present-day "Arabs" (both within and outside Palestine) have little ethnic and historical connection among themselves; in fact, they share only one thing: the Arabic language. There has never been a "Palestinian people" as a separate ethnic entity.

Explanation: The word "Palestine" is a Greek (*Palaistinē*) and later Roman (*Palaestina*) adaptation of the word "Philistea." The Arabic name for "Palestine" is *Filistin* (or *Falastin*), a word that can be traced back to the ancient biblical term *F'listim*, "Philistines." The term "Palestine" was introduced by the Romans from the year AD 70 (the year of the destruction of Jerusalem and the Jewish temple) and especially after the year 135 (the year the Romans suppressed the Jewish revolt of Shimon Bar Kochba). The Romans believed that when the Jews were largely expelled from the "Holy Land," or "the land of Israel," it should be called "Palestine" to erase the memory of the Jews. The inhabitants of that land were henceforth called "Palestinians," completely irrespective of whether they were of Roman or Greek, Turkish or Armenian, Jewish or Arab origin.

Before World War II, even the Jews who had settled in the Holy Land to rebuild that neglected land naturally referred to themselves as "Palestinians," residents of the land of Palestine. There were American Jews, European Jews, African Jews, and Palestinian Jews. Even the charter of the PLO (the Palestine Liberation Organization; see Thesis 3) states that Jews living in Palestine are "Palestinians." Under the British Mandate (see Thesis 3), the Jews had a "P" on their passports and were indeed referred to as "Palestinians.'

By using the term exclusively for the present-day *Arab* residents of Palestine, uninformed individuals are immediately led astray. This usage portrays Arab Palestinians as the true Palestinians and (falsely) suggests that Palestine belongs to the Arab Palestinians and to them alone. Supposedly, the Jews have no place there, as they are not Palestinians. This entire line of thought is based on deception (to a significant extent, *deliberate* deception, I might add).

One could say it like this: historically, there is no conflict between Jews and Palestinians. There is, however, a conflict between Jewish Palestinians and Arab Palestinians. This is a political and legal conflict, but most importantly, it's a religious conflict, as we will see. Those who don't have a clear understanding of several historical facts regarding this issue become hopelessly confused. Therefore, let's try to organize these facts.

THESIS 2

Arabic-speaking people (both Muslims and Christians) have been living in Palestine for many centuries. However, Jews have also been living there for centuries, and at some times and in some places, there were more Jews than Arabs in the land. Therefore, it is incorrect to claim that the land of Palestine belongs to the Arab Palestinians (especially the Muslims).

Explanation: It is a grave mistake to claim that "the" (Arabic-speaking) Palestinians have been living in Palestine for centuries, and that Jews are recent "intruders." Nothing could be further from the truth. *There have been Jews living in the Holy Land virtually continuously since the arrival of Israel under the leadership of Moses* (about 3,200 to 3,400 years ago). The Assyrians deported the ten tribes of Israel into exile, and the Babylonians did the same with the remaining two tribes (the kingdom of Judah), but the Jews returned. The Romans expelled them, but there were always Jews left behind, or they tenaciously returned. The (Christian!) Crusaders did their best to expel the Jews, but the Jews came back. Where else could they go in a world (Islamic or Christian) that was so hostile to them? The Holy Land had traditionally been their God-given safe haven, and it remains their homeland to this day. Even the Jews who have remained in the Americas or in Europe (or elsewhere) will generally readily admit that the land of Israel is their true homeland. A Jew traveling to Israel is not "visiting"; they are "coming home," even if their ancestors left the land centuries ago.

For centuries, the Jews have been primarily located in Israel's four holy cities:

- *Jerusalem* (the ancient walled city where they prayed to God at the so-called "Western Wall," the last remnant of the old temple complex);
- *Hebron* (where the Jews prayed at the graves of the Jewish patriarchs: Abraham and Sarah, Isaac and Rebekah, Jacob and Leah);
- *Tiberias* (where the Mishnah—the rabbinic commentary on the Torah—and the so-called Palestinian Gemara [commentary on the Mishnah] were produced);
- *Safed* (now called Tsfat), where Jewish "Kabbalists" (mystics) have formed a large community for centuries.

In summary: Israel has been living in the Holy Land for thousands of years, and Jerusalem has been their holiest city for thousands of years because the first and second temples stood there. The people of Israel have never been completely absorbed into the world of nations, and no one has ever been able to completely eradicate Israel, although this has been attempted many times. The fact that Israel has managed to preserve its identity is mainly due to Israel holding onto its religious identity (the Torah, circumcision, the Sabbath and the High Holidays, and dietary laws) throughout the ages.

For centuries, a part of the Jews has resided in the Holy Land. For over a century now, another significant part of Israel has returned to that land. No power in the world has ever succeeded in permanently expelling all Jews from the Holy Land, and that will not happen now either.

It is also remarkable that *there have been more Jews than Muslims living in Jerusalem for a long time*: in 1860, there were 11,000 Jews compared to 6,500 Muslims, and in 1906, there were 40,000 Jews compared to 7,000 Muslims. Jerusalem has always been more of a Jewish city than an Arab one at all times. Therefore, Palestinians cannot claim any "right" to (old) Jerusalem because the city has never been in their possession, let alone being their *capital*. While it may be the third holiest city for Muslims (see Thesis 11), it is the first and foremost holy city for Jews (and to some extent, also for Christians because Jesus Christ was crucified, buried, resurrected, and ascended to heaven there).

THESIS 3

Throughout all those centuries, there has never been such a thing as a "Palestinian state." There were only Palestinian Jews and Palestinian Arabs under Mamluk rule (until 1517), under Turkish rule (until 1920), under British rule (until 1948), and under Jordanian rule (until 1967). Additionally, the "Palestinians" in the Gaza Strip had Egyptian nationality, and those on the Golan Heights had Syrian nationality.

Explanation: For many centuries, there has not been an independent state in the Holy Land, neither a Jewish state nor an Arab state. In 1291, the Mamluks (Turkish-European, *non*-Arab slave-soldiers) expelled the last Crusaders from the Holy Land and established a Middle Eastern empire that extended from Eastern Turkey to Syria, including Palestine. In 1517, the Ottoman Empire (Turks ruled by the Ottoman dynasty) defeated the Mamluks. Now the Turks were in charge, even in Palestine, which lasted for an astonishing four hundred years.

During World War I, the British captured Jerusalem (1917), and from 1920, Palestine was part of the so-called British Mandate. The "mandate" was entrusted to the British by the United Nations to administer Palestine and Mesopotamia (modern-day Iraq) temporarily, just as the French received a similar "mandate" for Syria and Lebanon.

A "Palestinian state," meaning an Arab state within the boundaries of ancient Palestine, has never existed. That would have been challenging to accomplish since Jews had lived in that same area for centuries, and even centuries earlier than the Arabs. The only real "Palestinian state" that ever existed was the (Jewish) *Kingdom of Israel* under the kings David and Solomon (later split into the northern ten-tribe and the southern two-tribe kingdoms).

Under the British Mandate (which ended on May 15, 1948), many Jews streamed into Palestine, mainly between the World Wars. These Jews helped cultivate the land in Palestine, a land that had been completely neglected by the Arabs for centuries. This remarkable cultural development also attracted guest workers from surrounding countries, who learned Arabic in Palestine and thus assimilated into the Arab "Palestinian" community. However, these people were by no means descendants of the ancient Bedouins! I have personally known "Palestinians" of Greek, Armenian, and Egyptian origin.

It is not relevant to argue that there were also Polish, Dutch, and American Jews who moved to Palestine, because the only thing these immigrants had in common was their *Jewish* identity. The (Christian or Muslim) Greeks, Armenians, and Egyptians who settled in Palestine for their livelihood had *nothing* in common, except a desire for a better life and the acquisition of Arabic, which allowed them to join the Arab "Palestinians." But to speak of an ancient "Palestinian nation" is simply historical falsification. The Arabs in Palestine, most of whom were Muslims, considered themselves part of the entire Arab Muslim community in the Middle East. However, the idea of a "Palestinian people" as a separate entity between the Jordan River and the Mediterranean Sea is a recent invention. Palestinian nationalism first emerged after the establishment of the State of Israel, and especially after the Six-Day War, largely due to Yasser Arafat (1929–2004), leader of the PLO (Palestine Liberation Organization).

Just the term itself, *Liberation* Organization, has deceived many. Were the Arab Palestinians supposed to be "liberated'? From what? And by whom? History has shown the purpose of the term: the land of Palestine needed to be "liberated" from all Jews. Nowadays, we often hear the cry: *From the River to the Sea, Palestine must be free*—meaning all Jews must be expelled (or better yet, killed) from the land, only then will Palestine truly be "liberated." It's somewhat akin to fumigating a house to eliminate a mosquito infestation.

THESIS 4

Therefore, it is historical nonsense to claim that Israelis occupied "Palestinian territory" in 1967. What they did was essentially occupy the ex-Turkish/ex-British/ex-Jordanian territory, where both Palestinian Jews and Palestinian Arabs had lived for centuries, in self-defense. Land owned by Arabs in that area needed to be respected by Israelis, just as Arabs needed to respect the land acquired by Jews.

Explanation: Here too, we need to pay close attention to the confusing use of the words "Palestine" and "Palestinian." Palestine is the ancient land of Israel, the Holy Land. The current state of Israel is situated in Palestine. The West Bank is located in Palestine. The Gaza Strip is located in Palestine. And over this Palestine, Jews, Romans, Crusaders, Mamluks, Turks, and Britons have ruled, *but never Arab Palestinians*. Israel is not the "occupier" of "Palestinian" territory; it is the Arab Palestinians who "occupy" areas where Israelites, Romans, Crusaders, Mamluks, Turks, and Britons, and between 1948 and 1967 also Jordanians, ruled for centuries, but never Arab Palestinians. There is no historical, legal, or theological basis for the claim that Israel "occupied" land belonging to "Arab Palestinians" during the Six-Day War in 1967. These are areas where both Jews and Arabs have lived for centuries and have been under foreign rule for centuries.

Speaking of "occupation," no one ever mentions that during the war of 1948–1949 (the war of the neighboring Arab countries against Israel), the West Bank was annexed by the Jordanians, even though that territory had been assigned to Arab Palestinians in 1947 (see the next Thesis). Jordan tightly controlled the residents of the West Bank (they were even denied the right to vote), and Egypt maintained military command over the Gaza Strip.

There is much lament about Israel supposedly keeping the West Bank "occupied" for 56 years (which had historically been their land), but I have never heard of international protests against the Jordanians who occupied that exact same territory between 1948 and 1967 and subjected its inhabitants to more severe repression. However, these were also Arabs, and so it wasn't such a big deal—as long as it wasn't Jews settling in the West Bank.

THESIS 5

It is historical nonsense to allege that Israelis have consistently "prevented" the establishment of a Palestinian state. Following the United Nations decision (November 29, 1947), not only did the Jews establish their own state, but the Arabs also could have immediately established their own state in their allocated territory, just as the Jews did in theirs (May 1948). Under significant pressure from the surrounding Arab countries (who believed that the state of Israel would quickly be destroyed), they chose not to do so, and many may regret that decision to this day.

Explanation: During the "British Mandate" (1920–1948), British leaders were mostly sympathetic toward the Arabs; there were simply many more of them in the Middle East than Jews, and those Arabs had rich oil reserves in various countries. However, in Palestine, the Jews were growing both in number and military strength, and they increasingly became an obstacle for the British, while the Arab Palestinians were also becoming more vocal. As a result, the British took the complicated "Palestinian issue" to the United Nations. An independent

UN commission then created a partition plan and presented it to the UN General Assembly. In this plan, Israel was allocated one part (Galilee, Western Palestine, Southern Palestine), and the (Arab) Palestinians were assigned another part (the ancient Judea and Samaria on the "West Bank," the strip along the western bank of the Jordan River, including old Jerusalem, which was also to have a kind of "international status" due to its significance for Jews and Christians).

There was immense suspense among Jews and Christians worldwide. Would it really happen? Would the Jews be granted their own territory in the Holy Land again? On November 29, 1947, the General Assembly adopted this proposal with 33 votes in favor, 13 votes against, and 10 abstentions. There was jubilation among Jews and among those Christians who believed in the biblical promise of the land for Israel in the end times (the time just before the appearance of the Messiah). Prophecies were coming true! ("Replacement theologians" [see Thesis 16], however, assured Christians that the founding of the state of Israel had as little to do with biblical prophecies as the establishment of the state of Belgium in 1830.)

What people today would apparently like to forget is that the Palestinian Jews agreed to this partition plan, even though they had to give up a large part of the Holy Land, including old Jerusalem (along with the Western Wall and the Temple Mount). *At that time, the Jews would not have objected if the Arab Palestinians in their assigned area had established their own state.* However, while the Jews did indeed declare the "state of Israel" on May 14, 1948—one day before the expiration of the "British Mandate"—under the leadership of David Ben-Gurion and Chaim Weizmann, the Arab Palestinians staunchly refused to establish their own state.

Their refusal was partly due to strong pressure from the surrounding Arab countries. The reason was straightforward: *the Arabs* (both inside the Holy Land and beyond) *wanted the entire land.* In 1947/48, the Jews settled for a limited part, while the Arabs wanted it all. As a result, they immediately launched an overwhelming attack against the newly formed state of Israel—and lost that war, which is known as Israel's War of Independence (1948–1949). Israel retained its newly acquired territory, but due to their own actions, the Palestinian Arabs ended up with nothing. Often in life, those who want everything sometimes end up with nothing.

THESIS 6

In 1948, many Arabs left the area that included the state of Israel since May 14 of that year. Jews may have played a role in scaring them into leaving, but it was just as much the surrounding countries that frightened the Arab Palestinians. Moreover, these countries assured the Arab Palestinians that their departure would only be temporary because after defeating the state of Israel, they could return to their homes. That turned out to be a massive mistake.

Explanation: It's not easy to determine who or what was primarily responsible for the fact that around 700,000 Arab inhabitants of the newly established state of Israel left their homes and fled to the surrounding Arab countries (where their descendants often still reside in "refugee camps" under false promises that they would someday be allowed to return to their ancestral land). In part, the Jews themselves may have contributed to this Arab departure by intimidating them. But it was also the surrounding Arab countries that exerted pressure on the Arab inhabitants in the state of Israel to leave. The war was supposed to be brief, the Jews would be driven into the sea, and then all of Palestine would "once again" belong to the Arab Palestinians, allowing the displaced Arabs to return to their homes.

Note the word "again" in the previous sentence, which traces back to one of the many falsehoods in this entire narrative. *The Arab Palestinians had never owned the land of Palestine as a whole.*

In 1948–1949, the Arab Palestinians did not regain the land either. Israel won the War of Independence, and the Arabs who had fled or their descendants never had the opportunity to return home. Some of the blame is rightfully placed on Israel (even Israel's so-called "New Historians" have acknowledged that many Arabs had fled due to actions by Jews), but a significant portion of the blame is entirely unjust. The Arabs who fled or their descendants might better direct their grievances towards the surrounding Arab countries, who never fulfilled their promises and never intended to integrate the Palestinian Arabs from the refugee camps into their own societies. The most severe oppression of the Arab Palestinians occurs in these countries.

THESIS 7

In fact, while hundreds of thousands of Arabs fled the newly established state of Israel (and were placed in refugee camps to this day), there were also hundreds of thousands of Jews who were expelled from the surrounding Arab countries (and found a new and free home in the new state of Israel).

Explanation: It appears that about 700,000 Arabs fled the state of Israel. However, what opponents of Israel usually don't mention is that *around 850,000 Jews were expelled from the surrounding Arab countries*. These were Jews whose ancestors had often lived in those Arab countries for centuries. Their everyday language was Arabic, their culture was Arabic. They had lived in relative harmony with their Arab neighbors—until the armies of the countries where they lived attacked the newly established state of Israel, and the anger of the Arabs in those neighboring countries turned against the Jews who had been in their midst for so many centuries. Why is there so little emphasis on this? Why lament the 700,000 fleeing Arabs and not the 850,000 fleeing Jews?

For the Arabs who fled from Israel, only refugee camps were reserved in the countries of destination and this continues to this day. It's something you can expect from your like-minded individuals (Muslim Arabs). For the Jews who fled from the neighboring Arab countries, it was entirely different: they were welcomed with open arms in the state of Israel, the land where their distant ancestors had once lived as well. The sons and daughters of these Jews joined the IDF (Israel Defense Force, the Israeli Defense Army) and had to fight against the Arabs in whose midst their ancestors had lived, in 1956 (the Suez Crisis, or the Second Arab-Israeli War), in 1967 (Six-Day War), and in 1973 (Yom Kippur War).

THESIS 8

The Arabs in the state of Israel, even though they can be called *de facto* second-class citizens, if you will, have it economically and politically much better than the Palestinians in the mentioned refugee camps—and, in fact, even better than Arabs in neighboring countries.

Explanation: Of course, the Arabs who still live in Israel and even hold Israeli nationality are, in a sense, second-class citizens. Israel is explicitly a *Jewish* state. Can we not agree on this simple fact, please? There are enough Arab countries in the world, but there is only one Jewish state. There is only one country in the world where Jews are truly safe from discrimination and anti-Semitism, and that is the land where their ancestors have lived for more than three thousand years: the land of Israel.

But that's not all: Israel is also the only truly *democratic* country in the entire Middle East, the only country where real freedom of speech exists. Islam and democratic freedoms do not go together. But behold: in the state of Israel, Arab residents have the same democratic rights as Jewish residents. There have always been one or more

Arab political parties represented in the Israeli parliament, and there are also Arabs serving as judges in the Supreme Court. Of the more than 300 million Arabs in the Middle East and North Africa, less than half a percent are truly free, and they all live in Israel. There is no country in this part of the world where Arabs can express their opinions as freely as in the land of Israel, including their possibly sharp criticism of the government.

There is no country in the Middle East where Arabic speakers have as many rights as in the land of Israel. Even the so-called "Palestinian Authority" in the West Bank is not a democracy; no elections have been held since 2006, and Mahmoud Abbas (born in 1935) has effectively ruled for decades. In the Gaza Strip, Hamas is in charge; here, too, there is no democracy. Moreover, Hamas and the Palestinian Authority are bitter enemies of each other. It's ironic to say, but for Israel, the mutual hatred of the Palestinian rulers is only beneficial.

In many countries in the Middle East, the average Arab has a lower economic standard of living than in the state of Israel. Before the current war, thousands of Arabs from Gaza went to Israel every day to earn money for themselves and their families. They benefited from Israel while many of them cursed it at the same time.

A little understanding for this might well be in order, then. The Jewish Christian Baruch Maoz wrote: "The West Bank and the Gaza Strip ... were ruled with a firm, military hand; yet, this Israeli military administration was the most enlightened, the most generous of all military occupations the world has ever seen. In twenty years, the standard of living on the West Bank and in Gaza reached the highest average in the Middle East, except for [the state of] Israel. New industries were established, agriculture was promoted, and agricultural yields made great strides. Tens of thousands of Arab Palestinians were employed in Israel, and the government made continuous efforts to put an end to illegal employment, which paid shameful wages and offered no social security. *However, the emerging Palestinian national consciousness had no outlet.* Moreover, extensive contact with Israeli Jews exposed many Palestinians to a kind of arrogance that one would have thought Jews could never display towards other people." This last part also deserves to be mentioned.

THESIS 9

It is not true that the majority of Arab Palestinians would support the two-state solution; at most, they might support it as a temporary interim solution. The most consistent Muslims (such as represented by Hamas, Hezbollah, the Islamic Jihad, the rulers of Iran) do not want anything other than the destruction of the state of Israel (if not the people of Israel). Consistent but also more moderate Arab Muslims have never fundamentally recognized the state of Israel.

Explanation: Since the beginning of the existence of the *nation* [or people; Dutch *volk*] of Israel, the great powers have sought not only to defeat Israel but to destroy it. In the Book of Exodus, it was the Pharaoh of Egypt who tried to destroy Israel by killing all newborn boys. In the Book of Esther, it was the Agagite Haman—a kind of prime minister of the Persian Empire—who, through the Persian king, attempted to destroy all of Israel. In Psalm 83, it is the combined neighboring countries of Israel that not only oppose the country but want to obliterate the entire people (verse 5). Adolf Hitler wanted the same and actually succeeded in killing six million Jews (which was nearly forty percent of all Jews on earth at the time). The Mufti (Muslim leader) in Palestine during that period, Mohammed Said Haj Amin al-Husseini (ca. 1897–1974), had exactly the same goal; he was also a personal friend of Hitler (and, what many do not know, an uncle or close blood relative of Yasser Arafat).

After May 14, 1948, *not a single* Palestinian organization has ever recognized the legitimate existence of the state of Israel, apparently because the hope of Muslim Arabs has always been that the state (and the nation [or people, Dutch *volk*) of Israel could still be destroyed. Extreme Muslim organizations like Hamas, Hezbollah, and the rulers in Iran have even openly stated that they aim to destroy both the state and the people of Israel, sometimes even enshrining this in their statutes and charters. In contrast, Israelis and Jews, in general, *have never aimed to destroy the Arab Palestinians*. An example: the charter of Hamas, dated August 1988, states: "Palestine is an Islamic Waqf land [land subject to Islamic law] dedicated to Muslim generations until the Day of Judgment. This, or part of it, may not be sold; this, or part of it, may not be abandoned. Neither an Arab state, nor all Arab states, nor any king or president, nor all kings and presidents, nor any organization, whether Palestinian or Arab, has the right to do so.... There is no solution to the Palestinian problem except by Jihad [Holy War against the Jews]. Initiatives, proposals, and international conferences are all a waste of time and vain efforts."

Take another look at the above-mentioned IDF abbreviation: Israel's army is a *defense* force to protect against Arab (and possibly Iranian) aggression. It is not Israel who is the aggressor in the Middle East (although ignorant individuals try to convince us otherwise), but it is the Muslim Arabs.

THESIS 10

The international community accuses Israel of "colonialism" and "imperialism." This is an absurd historical distortion. It was Israel that agreed to the division of the land in 1947 and international status for Jerusalem. It is the Arabs who, instead of agreeing to this, have repeatedly waged war against Israel. The only time they managed to conquer old Jerusalem (1948/49), they immediately expelled all Jews from it.

Explanation: I need to address the claim here that Israel *initiated* the Six-Day War in June 1967. Strictly speaking, this is true, but it was only after all the Arab neighboring countries had massively mobilized against Israel. In June 1967, huge armies, vast numbers of tanks and planes were ready to finally destroy Israel. Israel successfully defended itself by launching a preemptive strike: it inflicted a massive military blow to the Arabs, effectively disabling a significant portion of the Arab military force.

Another absurd accusation is that Israel practices "apartheid." As if Arabs are forced to live in reservations! Jews have also not established a "colony" in Palestine; they have organized themselves as a state in a land that had been their own for centuries and where Jews had always lived since then with the permission of the United Nations, representing the international community.

However, it should be added that while Arab Palestinians cannot claim that Palestine was ever "their own" land, Palestinian families have undoubtedly lived in the land for centuries. That's why, in 1947, they were assigned their own area within the land of Palestine, where they could have established their own state—which they refused. This is no surprise: they openly admit that they would prefer to expel all Jews from the land, including Jews whose ancestors had lived there for many centuries. Palestinian mentality became apparent in the War of Independence in 1948–1949 when one of the few accomplishments of the Arabs was expelling all Jews from East Jerusalem. (They could return only in 1967.) After the establishment of the state of Israel, the Israelis have never attempted to expel all Arabs from their land, just as they have never attempted to expel all Arabs from East Jerusalem after 1967.

THESIS 11

The city of Jerusalem is not mentioned in the Quran at all. Instead, there is reference to the "utmost" or "farthest" mosque, which later generations of Muslims have projected onto Jerusalem (Al-Aqsa Mosque means "utmost" or "farthest" mosque). In the Quran or by later Muslim prophets, there has never been a (messianic) realm of peace and justice promised around Jerusalem for the Muslims, as it has been promised to Israel (a divine promise that is still in effect).

Explanation: Historically speaking, it is actually remarkable that Muslims have made the city of Jerusalem so important to them. Jerusalem is not mentioned in the Quran at all. As a *city*, Jerusalem is not important for traditional Islam. The only thing that is holy and thus important is the rock in the Dome of the Rock on the Temple Mount (referred to as Haram al-Sharif by Muslims), from where, according to Muslims, Muhammad made a night journey to heaven. This is alluded to in Surah 17:1: "Exalted is He who took His Servant by night from al-Masjid al-Haram to al-Masjid al-Aqsa." For world history, this supposed journey is of the utmost importance, as it led Muslims to think of Jerusalem when referring to the "farthest mosque." What could be more fitting than to imagine that the God of Muhammad had overshadowed the God of Israel (see Thesis 14) and that, therefore, the Temple Mount should be under Islamic control? Partly based on this pure speculation, Jerusalem became the third holy city of Islam—a fact that has had enormous political and religious consequences to this day.

However, it is important to note that the word "partly" should be emphasized. Indeed, Jerusalem was already so important to Muhammad that he initially instructed his followers to pray in the direction of Jerusalem (later changed to Mecca). After Muslims conquered Jerusalem in 638, Caliph Omar visited the Temple Mount, and in 691/2, the Dome of the Rock (sometimes mistakenly called the Omar Mosque) was built on that site. Around 711, Caliph Abd al-Malik converted the church built by Christians on the Temple Mount in the sixth century into a mosque, naming it Al-Aqsa Mosque to suggest that it was the "Farthest Mosque" (Al-Masjid al-Aqsa) from the Quran. However, there was no mosque ("place of worship") in Jerusalem during Muhammad's time! So Surah 17:1 (see the previous paragraph) cannot possibly refer to Jerusalem; Muhammad likely thought of Medina instead.

Meanwhile, Islam had triumphed over Judaism and Christianity in Jerusalem in this way. From then on, the holy mountain was theirs. It should be noted, though, that Muslims have shown little interest in the Temple Mount throughout the centuries. From the seventh century onwards, most caliphs and sultans scarcely concerned themselves with Jerusalem; by the nineteenth century, the city had become a filthy, impoverished place. There was little evidence that Jerusalem was the third holy city of Islam; only in the twentieth century did the emphasis on this change, for political reasons. It was only when Jews settled massively in and around Jerusalem that Muslims made Jerusalem an important city for themselves.

It is also noteworthy that throughout history, *there have always been more Jews than Muslims living in Jerusalem*. In 1860, when Zionism did not yet exist, there were 11,000 Jews compared to 6,500 Muslims, and in 1906, there were 40,000 Jews compared to 7,000 Muslims. At all times, Jerusalem has been more of a Jewish city than an Arab one. However, this fact is rarely mentioned in the media. "Jerusalem belongs to the Palestinians"—that cry is much more popular among thoughtless individuals.

THESIS 12

Israel's settlement policy has often been heavily criticized. However, these settlements (a) only exist in the so-called C-zone, which is the zone where Israel (with the consent of the Palestinians at the time!) has full civil and military control since the Oslo Accords (1993–1995); and (b) the relevant territories are not stolen from "the" Palestinians but are honestly purchased from Arab Palestinians. (Whether this was always done so neatly in practice, I will leave aside for now.)

Explanation: Once again, it is of the utmost importance to emphasize that there has never been an area that was exclusively Arab-Palestinian, and there is none today. That would have been very different if the Arabs had established their own state in their allotted part in 1948, but they deliberately refrained from doing so. Moreover, under the leadership of Yasser Arafat, the Palestinians themselves accepted the division of the West Bank into three zones during the Oslo Accords (1993–1995):

- The A-zone (urban area, especially around Ramallah, Jericho, Nablus, and Jenin) is entirely under the jurisdiction of the Palestinian Authority;
- The B-zone is under the authority of the Palestinian Authority but is also under Israeli military control to ensure the security of the area;
- The C-zone is under Israeli control (even though it does not belong to the state of Israel).

The Palestinians themselves agreed with this division, under the watchful eye of the whole world. In the C-zone, Jews have purchased land from Arab Palestinians—not stolen or seized—and established Jewish settlements there. You can have your opinions on this, and you can also question whether the establishment of these settlements always followed the rules strictly. Just do not claim that Israelis have "illegally" acquired "Palestinian" (read: Muslim-Arab) territory.

In fact, the same thing is happening in the West Bank as occurred throughout all of Palestine between the First and Second World Wars. During that time, Jews from all over the world flocked to Palestine and bought land from Arabs. This land often consisted of swamps and other complete wilderness areas. What the Jewish pioneers did was bring that land back into cultivation after centuries of neglect. Many Palestinians envied the great success that Jews achieved in these projects, but other Palestinians were happy to help with these projects for payment and benefited significantly for their own agriculture, partly thanks to the generous assistance of many Jewish farmers. In many places in Palestine at the time, Jews and Arabs interacted reasonably harmoniously and even worked together, and here and there, this still happens in the West Bank (something that Israel's enemies prefer to ignore). Jews and Arabs can coexist in harmony; they have done so in Palestine for many centuries. The most disturbing factor here is not politics but religion.

To understand the mysterious point of how the Palestinians ever agreed to the Oslo Accords, you must be aware of an important aspect of Islam. Even in the Ottoman Empire, it was common practice for Muslim leaders, when their political power was inferior to that of non-Muslim rulers, to focus on *mudara*, "cat-friendliness," until the balance of power shifted in their favor again. Islam also practices *iham*, the systematic deception of the "enemies of Allah" in dealing with them. The Oslo Accords were nothing more than a temporary break in hostilities (a *hudna* or a *muwada'a*) as a tactical means of political weakness. After signing these accords, Arafat is said to have remarked, "I consider this agreement to be nothing more than the agreement that was signed between our Prophet Muhammad and the Quraysh [tribe]." Two years after Muhammad signed a peace treaty (the Treaty of Hudaybiyya, 628) with the anti-Islam Quraysh, he attacked this tribe and inflicted a severe defeat on them.

According to Sharia, Islamic law, the Oslo Accords should not even be taken seriously; it is the religious duty of Muslims to break them as soon as the opportunity arises. During the Fourth Conference of the Islamic Research Academy in Cairo (1968), the highest Islamic legal scholar in Jordan said, "Peace resolutions are permitted to gather strength only for future conflicts in times of weakness. The holy war [jihad] must be the basis of relations between Muslims and non-Muslims. Muslims are free to break any agreement with non-Muslims." Here it is clear that in the Middle East, it is a spiritual struggle, a battle between the God of Israel and Allah, the god of Islam. This makes the problem much more serious, which the next statement addresses.

THESIS 13

The deepest issue in and around the state of Israel is not of historical, political, or international legal nature but of a religious nature. Since the conquest of Palestine in the seventh century, it is inconceivable for consistent Muslims that a Jewish state would exist there. What has become the "land of Allah" can never be given back to Jews. Conversely, for devout Jews, it is inconceivable to live anywhere other than in the land promised to their forefathers by God.

Explanation: It is astonishing how many so-called experts on Palestine—often including Jews and Christians—overlook the profound religious dimension of the entire Jewish-Palestinian conflict. Palestine is the land that the God of Israel once gave to Israel. In that Holy Land, Jerusalem was the holy city, and Zion was the holy mountain where Israel's holy temple was built (first Solomon's temple, later Zerubbabel's temple). Each year, on the ninth day of the month of Av, Israel still mourns the loss of its two temples, and religious Jews in the Diaspora (dispersion) still pray at *Passover* [*Pesach*]: "Next year in Jerusalem" (and the Jews already living in Jerusalem pray,

"Next year in the new temple"). For religious Jews, the land of Israel is still the Holy Land, and even for many secularized Jews, the land of Israel remains their historical homeland.

The Holy Land of Muslims is Saudi Arabia—not Palestine—and mainly Mecca and Medina. But in a mysterious way, as mentioned earlier, Muslims have made Jerusalem their third holy city. Furthermore, Muslims conquered Palestine in the seventh century, and since then, that land has belonged to the "realm of Allah." Today, the world is still divided into two regions: the *dar al-islam*, the "house of Islam," where the majority of the population is Muslim, and the *dar al-harb*, the "house of war," where the majority of the population is not yet Muslim. The first "house" must subdue (Islamize; *Islam* means "submission") the second "house," if possible through peaceful means or else by force. Once all people have become Muslims, the world will be *dar al-salaam*, the "house of peace." This is the Islamic concept of "peace," which involves Islamizing all opponents (subjecting them to slavish submission to Allah or *Sharia*, Islamic law).

The fact that organizations like Hamas and Hezbollah want to destroy Israel is not simply based on anti-Semitism or hatred of Jews (although that is also true). There is this deeply religious component: Jews can live in Muslim areas (in strict submission), but it is inconceivable that Jews would ever have their own state in an area that has become part of Allah's world. This is an abomination to many consistent Muslims, both within and outside the Middle East. For seventy-five years, these Muslims have fervently desired that the state of Israel come to an end as soon as possible.

THESIS 14

The religious depth dimension of the Jewish-Palestinian conflict was evident on October 7, 2023, when Hamas members assaulted, raped, and murdered 1,400 Jews while continually shouting: Allahu Akbar, which, in this case, meant something like: "Our god Allah is greater than the God of Israel!" Nothing could more clearly illustrate that this was and still is a battle in the heavenly realms (cf. Ephesians 6:12): a struggle between the "gods" of this world and the God of Israel.

Explanation: Originally, Allahu Akbar meant something like: "Allah is greater than the heathen idols." However, in the battle of Muslims against Jews and also against Christians, the cry increasingly meant: "Allah is greater (and hence more powerful) than the God of Jews and Christians," and thus also: ultimately, the god of Muslims will triumph over all the gods of the world, including the God of Jews and Christians.

I myself have heard hundreds of Muslims shouting the same thing at orthodox Jews passing by on the Temple Mount in Jerusalem: Allahu Akbar, "Allah is greater than your God." In that fanatical, frightening cry, I could almost hear the following: You, Jews, do not belong on this mountain! This mountain belongs to our god! And one day we will finally drive you out of this part of the world, and then our god will triumph on this mountain! Our god has the final word!

Israel's struggle against its enemies has been governed by the same principles since the beginning of its history. When Israel was about to depart from Egypt, very much against Pharaoh's wishes, God said to Israel, "I will execute judgments on all the gods of Egypt" (Exodus 12:12; see the fulfillment in Numbers 33:4). Not so much judgments on Pharaoh—that too—but especially on the dark spiritual powers behind Pharaoh.

The conflict between Israel and the Babylonian empire also involved a battle of the God of Israel against the gods of Babylon: Bel, Nebo, Marduk (cf. Isaiah 46:1; Jeremiah 51:44). Then there was the struggle of Israel against the "gods" (angelic rulers) of the Persian and Greek-Macedonian empires (Daniel 10:13, 20).

These "gods" are actually demonic angelic powers that have turned against the "God of gods" (Deuteronomy 10:17; Daniel 2:47; 11:36) but are in fact "dragons" (demonic monsters). Compare Isaiah 27:1 and 51:9, and especially the "dragon" in the Book of Revelation, the angelic ruler of the world power of the end times, who will have to contend with the God of Israel and particularly the Messiah of Israel. From the Exodus from Egypt to the present, the battle is between the God of Israel and the spiritual powers of darkness.

I once said to a rabbi friend in Jerusalem, "Anti-Semitism is proof of the existence of God." He understood me immediately. What I meant is that anti-Semitism points to a spiritual power that goes beyond normal understanding. The existence of such a power suggests a spiritual force against which that malevolent power is directed. We call that spiritual power God.

Here is a simple example of this spiritual power: in 2014, the Israeli ambassador Ron Prosor said the following at the United Nations General Assembly, among other things: "When members of the international community talk about the Israeli-Palestinian conflict, a fog descends that obscures all logic and moral clarity. The result is not realpolitik but surrealpolitik. The world's relentless focus on the Israeli-Palestinian conflict is an injustice to tens of millions of victims of tyranny and terrorism [by Arabs and Iranians] in the Middle East. As we speak, Yazidis, Bahai, Kurds, Christians, and Muslims are being killed and expelled by radical extremists at a rate of a thousand people per month. How many resolutions did you pass last week to address this crisis? And how many special sessions did you request for this problem? The answer is zero. What does this say about the international concern for human life? Not much, but it speaks volumes about the hypocrisy of the international community."

During all those years, the United Nations has adopted numerous resolutions against Israel but never one against Muslim terrorism. What kind of power is behind this?

THESIS 15

Pay attention to the "objectivity" of the media (or the lack thereof): it is *correct* to emphasize that Israel in Gaza primarily targets only Hamas targets, even though unfortunately, many civilians are also affected; there is simply no war without civilian casualties. This is largely the fault of Hamas itself, which prefers to use innocent civilians as human shields, for example, by hiding in or under hospitals and schools. However, it is entirely *incorrect* to focus solely on the innocent civilians affected by Israel and even give the impression that Israel is deliberately targeting those civilians. Thus, Israel continues to be portrayed as the villain, as it has been throughout the centuries.

Explanation: Rarely have I felt so "tired" when reading and listening to what the media generally has to say about the Israel-Hamas conflict. *I*, too, find it terrible that so many civilians, especially children, are killed in Gaza. But that is precisely the devilish dilemma that the government of Israel is wrestling with: either spare the civilians of Gaza, thereby sparing Hamas as well (allowing them to prepare for the next attack on innocent Jews); or go all out to destroy Hamas in Gaza, even if it costs the lives of many civilians.

How many media outlets provide an unbiased perspective on this dilemma? How many media outlets focus exclusively on all those "innocent" civilians "murdered" by Israel (some even speak of "genocide'), instead of emphasizing that Israel can scarcely act any differently as long as Hamas continues to hold about two hundred innocent Jews (and foreigners) hostage? Why does "someone" see one side of the matter so easily and the other side so reluctantly? Why do even many Christians participate in these kinds of distortions?

I am in fact rather cautious with the term "innocent" civilians. In 2007, those civilians in Gaza themselves brought Hamas to power. Also, many civilians in Gaza must be aware of the ways in which Hamas fighters hide among them. At the same time, I understand (a) that the Gazans in 2007 did not have much choice, (b) that many Gazans do not agree with the policies of Hamas, and (c) they also cannot help that Hamas uses them as human shields. That is the dilemma precisely: the dilemma of the Israelis but also the dilemma of the Gazans.

It is in fact equally true that many Gazans are just as anti-Israel as other Arab Palestinians. This is sometimes the fault of Israel itself—Jews are God's people, but by no means a perfect people—but it is mainly inherent in the nature of Islam (see the next proposition).

THESIS 16

There are indeed Muslims who have a favorable attitude towards many Jews. But fundamentally, every devout Muslim is an Israel hater. The Prophet Mohammed tried to exterminate the Jewish tribes in his region during his time because they would not follow him. It is true that the early parts of the Quran contain benevolent words about the Jews, but later parts of the Quran have more authority according to Muslims than those earlier parts. The overall trend of those later parts is a strict condemnation of the Jews: "Allah has cursed them for their disbelief" (Surah 2:88); He is "angry" with them (58:14) and has destined them for hell (59:3).

Explanation: I would like to add: Surah 5:51 says: "O you who believe [i.e., Muslims], do not take the Jews and the Christians as allies; they are [in fact] allies of one another. And whoever is an ally to them among you - then indeed, he is [one] of them." Surah 9:123 says: "O you who have believed, fight those adjacent to you of the disbelievers [i.e., Jews and Christians] and let them find in you harshness." These and other verses are often explained away by Muslims who want to present a friendly image to the outside world. In reality, these verses make it clear what Jihad (the "holy war" of Muslims) ultimately is: the ultimate goal of Islam is to bring the entire world under submission to the Quran, *whatever the cost* (see Thesis 13).

For that, all Jews who stand in the way must yield. Already in the late nineteenth century, thousands of Jews were killed throughout the Muslim world, simply because they were Jews. During the period surrounding the Second World War, more than a thousand Jews were killed in anti-Jewish riots in Muslim countries. Permanent peace between Jews and Muslims is therefore fundamentally difficult on a collective, political level. However, permanent peace between a Jewish state (on former Islamic territory!) and its Muslim neighboring states is completely out of the question.

Mohammed himself began to hate the Jews with a burning hatred when it became clear that the Jews of his time would not accept his message. In May 627, according to certain sources, he had almost all Jewish men in Medina (the Banu Qurayza tribe) slaughtered; the women and children were sold as slaves. In a four-year war (624–628), Mohammed defeated all the Jewish tribes living in Arabia. Many Jews were killed or expelled, and the rest were plundered and made subject to tribute, with many possessions destroyed. In 640, Caliph Omar expelled the last Jews from Arabia. No Muslim—and indeed, no Jew—can forget Mohammed's hatred of the

Jews. Even though Islam has had times when Muslims and Jews lived together fairly peacefully (especially in medieval Spain), wherever Jews obstruct Islam again, as is currently the case in the land of Israel, old hatred resurfaces.

The American historian and journalist John Laffin († 2000) wrote: "If even Mohammed was justified in killing Jews, the same could be said of Muammar al-Qaddafi, Yasser Arafat, and President Sadat" (former presidents of Libya, the Palestinian Authority, and Egypt, respectively)—and the same can be said of Hamas, Hezbollah, the Iranian rulers, and so on. They are the ones "in whom the god of this age [i.e., the current era] has blinded the minds of the unbelievers" (2 Corinthians 4:4).

Hamas spokesperson Ibrahim Ghoseh in Amman wrote in 1992: "Compromise is not possible. Muslims do not recognize the Zionist entity, in whatever form it takes." Only naive Westerners, who misunderstand the religious depth of the conflict, can believe in a two-state solution. These are either unbelievers or Christians who want to view the matter solely from a legal or political perspective, or Christians who adhere to "replacement theology" (the theology that holds that the Church has taken over the role and blessings and promises of Israel, and thus, in today's Israel, none of the biblical prophecies are being fulfilled).

With regard to this latter item: among Palestinian Christians, there is a huge difference between, on the one hand, the traditional "replacement theology" viewpoint (such as Greek Orthodox, Roman Catholics, and traditional Protestants) and, on the other hand, evangelical Christians who do believe in the validity of the biblical land promise and love Israel as the people of God (even if they understandably do not always agree with the Israeli leaders). "The" Palestinian Christians do not exist. Thus, when asking a Palestinian Christian for their opinion, it must first be determined whether that Christian subscribes to "replacement theology" or believes in the continuing validity of the biblical land promise for Israel. This applies to Dutch Christians as well. Take, for example, the Protestant Church in the Netherlands (PKN): there is no "PKN stance" on the Israel-Palestine conflict. People might talk about a "connection" with Israel, but that is an empty term; it can also mean the historical connection with the ancient people of Israel. Both the liberals and the "replacement theologians" within the PKN want nothing to do with the ongoing validity of the biblical land promise for Israel. Every Christian discussion about the Israel-Palestine conflict should therefore begin with this question: do you believe in the ongoing validity of the biblical land promise or not? The answer to that question determines the entire discussion in advance.

THESIS 17

Thus, there is *absolutely no* conceivable political or international legal solution for the Israeli-Palestinian problem. The Arab Muslim world will fundamentally never be able and willing to recognize a state of Israel, and the Israelis will never be able and willing to give up their settlement policy, nor take back the hundreds of thousands of refugees in Arab camps. Neither party will ever be willing to give up old Jerusalem and the Temple Mount. Therefore, we are waiting for the coming of the Messiah and—from Jerusalem—the establishment of His world empire of peace and justice. As a Christian-Arab taxi driver in Jerusalem once said to me: Only Jesus can solve the problem.

Explanation: I could not think of any political problem on Earth for which, in principle, there should not be a political solution. Except for the Jewish-Palestinian conflict. This is due to its religious depth, which is not found to the same extent in other issues (e.g., the war between Russia and Ukraine). Just consider this one point: many Arab Palestinians have personally told me that they are in favor of a two-state solution—but only if (old) Jerusalem becomes its capital (and that, while Jerusalem has never been the capital of an Arab Palestinian state). Many Jewish Israelis have told me that they are also in favor of a two-state solution—but only if (old) Jerusalem becomes its capital (and that, while old Jerusalem was not part of the part of Palestine assigned to the Jews in 1947). Well, that makes it very difficult: neither party will ever accept a solution without old Jerusalem—and for deeply religious reasons.

Also, the time is long past when the two parties would accept some kind of "international status" for Jerusalem. After all, who would guard that "status"? This would soon lead to a new war.

Again, for Muslims, the Holy Land is non-negotiable because it has been the "land of Allah" since the seventh century, which can never be entirely or partially gifted to non-Muslims. And for Jews, the Holy Land is non-negotiable because it is God's land ("the land is Mine", Leviticus 25:23), which He promised and gave to His people Israel and to no one else. Therefore, no conflict in the world can be "more religious" than this struggle for the Holy Land and the holy city and the holy mountain. I repeat: it can only be understood by Bible believers who see the struggle in the "heavenly realms" (Ephesians 6:12): the struggle between the "dragon" and the "Lamb" (as described in the Book of Revelation), between the "gods" of this world and the God of Israel (who is also the God of Christians).

THESIS 18

I do not justify everything that the current state of Israel is doing (as some claim); on the contrary, a large segment of today's Israelis is thoroughly secular and acts accordingly. But that was also the case in earlier times when God never ceased to be the God of Israel and never revoked any of His promises to Israel.

Explanation: God is still the God of Israel—although He has also become the God of millions of Christians, as He is, in a sense, the God of all people. God is the God who will never be able or willing to go back on His promises to Israel (cf. Romans 11:29).

It must be added that the fulfillment of God's promises to Israel always involves repentance and conversion on the part of Israel. We see this today in "Messiah-believing" (Jesus-believing) Jews (as I understand it, there are about 15,000 in Israel today), but also in genuinely pious "orthodox" (Talmudic) Jews, even though these latter still have a veil over their faces regarding Jesus (2 Corinthians 3:15-16). For many, this will change only when they see the Messiah appear with the clouds of heaven (Revelation 1:7). Just as Joseph's brothers recognized him only when he revealed himself to them (Genesis 45), so it will be with many Jews, who will recognize Jesus when He reveals Himself to them.

In that future time, the veil covering the faces of Christians will also be removed (cf. Isaiah 25:7). After all, the blind spot of many Jews consists of Jesus—but the blind spot of many Christians consists of Israel. I look forward to the time when both veils will be removed! That will be the time when the great sabbath peace will have arrived for the whole world (cf. Isaiah 9:6; Hebrews 4:9).

THESIS 19

God's land promise to Israel is inviolable. God has explicitly promised that the Israelites would one day return to the land where their forefathers once lived (Deuteronomy 30:5; 1 Kings 8:34; Jeremiah 30:3; Ezekiel 20:42), not to some spiritual or heavenly "land." The fact that this promise does not pertain (solely) to the return from the Babylonian exile is evident from the fact that it concerns a return from all the countries of the world (Isaiah 5:26) and is linked to the coming of the Messiah and the establishment of His reign (see, for example, Jeremiah 30-33; Ezekiel 34-48).

Explanation: With a thesis like this, we must always remember that there are also God's promises for the Arab Palestinians! For many Christians, accepting the literal land promise for Israel is already challenging; how does it work then with God's promises for *Ishmael*?

Although the Arab Palestinians, for the most part, have come from other countries in the last century and a half, with Greek, Armenian, Turkish, Central Asian, and North African blood in their veins, I assume that most of them can still consider the biblical Ishmael as their forefather. The sons of Keturah have also contributed to their DNA (Genesis 25:1–4), but it is my opinion that it is not an exaggeration to consider the Arab Bedouin tribes as descendants of Ishmael.

Descendants of Ishmael have a special place in God's plans, just as Ishmael held a special place in the book of Genesis, almost as significant as the three patriarchs (Abraham, Isaac, and Jacob). Ishmael is a type of Israel according to the flesh (cf. Genesis 17:20; Galatians 4:1–7): a "wild donkey" (a wild lawless one; Genesis 16:12), who ultimately must be redeemed by a Lamb (Exodus 13:13)—but God has provided for him in His providence (Genesis 17:20), and He has done so up to this day. Thus, there was divine grace not only for Israel but also for Hagar and Ishmael; we even read, "God was with the boy [Ishmael]" (Genesis 21:20).

Ultimately, it was Isaac and Ishmael who *together* buried their father Abraham (Genesis 25:11–18). This event was a precursor to the peace that will reign between Israel and the Arabs in the coming Messianic reign when the Abrahamic covenant will have found its complete fulfillment.

THESIS 20

In addition to similarities between Ishmael and Isaac, there are also significant differences: the line of God's covenant continues with Isaac, not with Ishmael. What is very characteristic is that Ishmael became a fighter (a slayer, just like Esau; Genesis 21:20), not a herder (feeder, caretaker) like Isaac. Ishmael took an Egyptian wife (Genesis 21:22), so all his descendants had that "Egyptian" in them. Israel, on the other hand, was formed as a people in Egypt but was allowed during the desert journey to learn to rid themselves of everything Egyptian (including the golden calf; Exodus 32–33). (Whether this was ever completely successful is another question.)

Explanation: Ishmael is included in God's promises. But Ishmael's descendants will not submit willingly to the God and Messiah of Israel; they never have. The prophet Isaiah speaks several times of the "Philistines" (again: the same word as "Palestinians"!) in a negative sense. This applies not only to the past but also to the end times. Isaiah 11 describes the peace of the Messianic kingdom (verses 1–9), but this state of peace is preceded by a conflict with the Palestinians in the west (the Gaza Strip!), as well as with Edom, Moab, and Ammon; in other words, Israel's neighboring countries.

Isaiah 60 is one of the special *positive* prophecies about the future of "Ishmael" and his place in the Messianic kingdom. While the name Ishmael is not mentioned, the names of his sons Kedar and Nebaioth (Genesis 25:13; 1 Chronicles 1:29) are mentioned, and various tribes of the Arabian Peninsula are listed (verse 6). It is (especially) the Ishmaelites who will help rebuild Jerusalem (verse 10). Many Ishmaelites will convert to the God and Messiah of Israel and be led by the light shining from Zion (verse 3).

Yes, you heard correctly: it is *Arab Palestinians* who will restore Jerusalem to its former glory in the Messianic kingdom. But they will do this for the God and Messiah of Israel, in whom they will learn to believe and whom they will serve themselves.

Ezekiel 47:21–23 is also very remarkable. In the Messianic kingdom, the Holy Land must be divided among the twelve tribes of Israel. *But also the "foreigners"* (i.e., non-Israelites) *who live among the Israelites and have children among them* (thus, those who are now called Arab Palestinians) *must also receive a share!* They will be on a par with natural born Israelites and will receive an inheritance in the Holy Land, just like the Israelites. This can happen only if they learn to submit to the God of Israel and the Messiah of Israel. This is precisely what Bible-believing Christian Palestinians are doing already today!

I know this because I have preached in Christian Palestinian congregations at least thirteen times, both within the state of Israel and on the West Bank, and have stayed with Palestinians in both areas.

Any Jew and any Christian who hates "Palestinians" because they are "Palestinians" is directly opposing God's plans. We must see Muslims primarily as people whom God loves, and whom we also must love. The fact that Israel is God's people does not mean that we should or may love Israelis more than Palestinians. This is especially true for a very practical reason: according to some missionary organizations, thousands of Muslims are coming to Christ today. We must learn to see in the face of every Muslim a potential Jesus-believer. Yes, one day (believing) Arabs will take an honored place alongside (believing) Jews in the kingdom of peace and justice under the blessed rule of Jesus Christ, the Messiah of Israel, who will sit on the throne of His father David (cf. Luke 1:32) in restored Jerusalem. Then the words of the prophet Isaiah will also be fulfilled:

> Sing a new song to the LORD,
> > sing His praise, all who live in the farthest corners of the earth.
>
> Sing, O sea!
> > Sing, all who live in far-off lands!
>
> The desert and its cities will be jubilant,
> > *the cities that Kedar [son of Ishmael!] inhabits* (Isaiah 42:10-11).

AFTERWORD

Allow me to conclude with the story of the Palestinian Taysir Abu Saada (Tass Saada), whose two books have been translated into Dutch and whom I have personally known. Tass is a former Muslim terrorist. He was born in a refugee camp in the Gaza Strip, grew up in Saudi Arabia and Qatar, worked as a driver for Yasser Arafat, and served as a sniper in the PLO. In the United States, he found the love of his life: Christ, the Jew who loves Arabs as much as Jews and who completely turned Saada's life around. He experienced a radical conversion, had the opportunity to explain the gospel to his own family and even to Yasser Arafat, began helping the poor and needy in Gaza and the West Bank and sharing the gospel with them. What he never could have imagined happened: he asked Israelis for forgiveness for what he and other Palestinians had done to them and learned to pray, "O God, bless Your people Israel. Lord, bring them back to the Promised Land. Show them that You are their God." In the face of the "spirit of terror" in the Middle East, Saada learned to be a peacemaker and to pray for those who sow death and destruction (on either side).

The same God who miraculously converted Saada also opened his eyes to God's plans for Israel. He writes: "[I] realized that I had fought in the wrong war. You Israelis have a right to this land, and I had no right to steal your rightful inheritance." And: "By reading the Bible, I am convinced that God wants the Jews to live in this land. He promised it to them a long time ago through His prophets, and He has never changed His mind. If we try to force them out, we are fighting against God. That is why we Arabs have never succeeded in defeating Israel, despite our vast numbers, oil dollars, and everything else." But Saada goes on: "... the truth is that God loves Arabs and Jews alike—and He wants to bring both of us to a higher purpose. He is not "against" one or the other. He wants all the peoples of the Middle East to realize that Jesus is their Savior and Reconciler."

Tass Saada is one of the many Muslims who have come to faith in Jesus Christ, especially since 9/11 (September 11, 2001, the Muslim attack on America)—if I can believe Joel Rosenberg, more of them than ever before in the history of Islam. Rosenberg is the founder of The Joshua Fund, a humanitarian organization with a mission to bless Israel and its neighbors in the name of Jesus based on Genesis 12:1–3. Saada himself is the founder of Hope for Ishmael, an organization that seeks to reconcile Arabs and Jews. His story is, in a way, the key to the booklet that the reader has in their hands: the only solution to the Middle East conflict is Jesus Christ—not merely faith in Him, but His return on the Mount of

Olives. The solution is not that Jews and Arabs are reconciled with each other because that is impossible under current conditions (with very enlightened exceptions). The solution is for Jews and Arabs to be reconciled with God individually, in Jesus Christ (2 Corinthians 5:18–20). Then reconciliation with each other will follow naturally (Ephesians 2:11–22).

Once again, here is the prophet Isaiah:

Arise, shine, for your light has come,
> and the glory of the LORD has risen upon you.

For behold, darkness shall cover the earth,
> and thick darkness the peoples;

but the LORD will arise upon you,
> and his glory will be seen upon you.

And nations shall come to your light,
and kings to the brightness of your rising.
Lift up your eyes all around, and see;
> they all gather together, they come to you;

your sons shall come from afar,
> and your daughters shall be carried on the hip.

Then you shall see and be radiant;
> your heart shall thrill and exult,

because the abundance of the sea shall be turned to you,
> the wealth of the nations shall come to you.

A multitude of camels shall cover you,
> the young camels of Midian and Ephah;
> all those from Sheba shall come.

> They shall bring gold and frankincense,
>> and shall bring good news, the praises of the
>> Lord.
> All the flocks of Kedar shall be gathered to you;
>> the rams of Nebaioth shall minister to you;
> they shall come up with acceptance on my altar,
>> and I will beautify my beautiful house.
> Who are these that fly like a cloud,
>> and like doves to their windows?
> For the coastlands shall hope for me,
>> the ships of Tarshish first,
> to bring your children from afar,
>> their silver and gold with them,
> for the name of the Lord your God,
>> and for the Holy One of Israel,
>> because he has made you beautiful.
> Foreigners shall build up your walls,
>> and their kings shall minister to you;
> for in my wrath I struck you,
>> but in my favor I have had mercy on you.
> Your gates shall be open continually;
>> day and night they shall not be shut,
> that people may bring to you the wealth of the nations,
>> with their kings led in procession.
> For the nation and kingdom
>> that will not serve you shall perish;
>> those nations shall be utterly laid waste.
> The glory of Lebanon shall come to you,

> the cypress, the plane, and the pine,
> to beautify the place of my sanctuary,
> > and I will make the place of my feet glorious.
> The sons of those who afflicted you
> > shall come bending low to you,
> and all who despised you
> > shall bow down at your feet;
> they shall call you the City of the LORD,
> > the Zion of the Holy One of Israel.
> Whereas you have been forsaken and hated,
> > with no one passing through,
> I will make you majestic forever,
> > a joy from age to age.
> You shall suck the milk of nations;
> > you shall nurse at the breast of kings;
> and you shall know that I, the LORD, am your Savior
> > and your Redeemer, the Mighty One of
> > Jacob.
>
> > > > > (Isaiah 60:1-16).

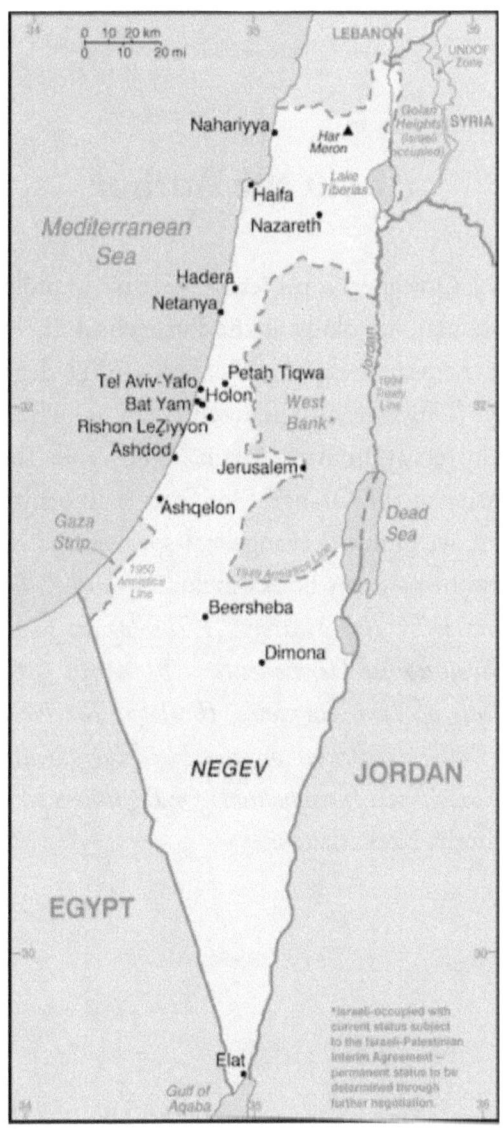

Land in the lighter shade represents territory within the borders of Israel at the conclusion of the 1948 war. This land is internationally recognized as belonging to Israel.

About the Author

Willem J. Ouweneel is professor emeritus of philosophy and systematic theology at the Evangelical Theological Faculty, Leuven, Belgium. He holds PhD degrees in Biology (University of Utrecht, 1970), Philosophy (Free University in Amsterdam, 1986) and Theology (University of the Orange Free State in Bloemfontein, 1993). A well-known evangelical speaker and debater, Dr. Ouweneel's many books include *Adam, Where Are You? And Why This Matters: A Theological Evaluation of the Evolutionist Hermeneutic*, *The World is Christ's: A Critique of Two Kingdoms Theology*, *The Heidelberg Diary: Daily Devotions on the Heidelberg Catechism*, and the *Academic Introductions for Beginners* series. He resides in the Netherlands.

FOR FURTHER READING

All the above theses and explanations can be better understood by the reader if they take the time to explore my comprehensive book *The Eternal People: God In Relation to Israel: Post-New Testament Israel* (vol. IV/1B of "An Evangelical Introduction to Reformational Theology" (Jordan Station, ON, Canada: Paideia Press, 2020), particularly Chapter 9, "Israel and the Palestinians." In that book, numerous references to other relevant publications are available. The sources for many of the theses I have discussed here and the quotes from others are also mentioned in the book.

(Translation assistance received from OpenAI. [2023]. ChatGPT Dutch-English translation. https://www.openai.com/chatgpt)

www.ingramcontent.com/pod-product-compliance
Lightning Source LLC
Chambersburg PA
CBHW032048290426
44110CB00012B/1008

9780888153456